Presented To

_____

_____

_____

_____

FROM

_____

_____

_____

DATE

_____

The Touch of Grace

One-Minute Nuggets for Emotional Healing and Inspiration

Jonathan Musvosvi

TEACH Services, Inc.
P U B L I S H I N G
www.TEACHServices.com • (800) 367-1844

World rights reserved. This book or any portion thereof may not be copied or reproduced in any form or manner whatever, except as provided by law, without the written permission of the publisher, except by a reviewer who may quote brief passages in a review.

The author assumes full responsibility for the accuracy of all facts and quotations as cited in this book.

The opinions expressed in this book are the author's personal views and interpretations, and do not necessarily reflect those of the publisher.

This book is provided with the understanding that the publisher is not engaged in giving spiritual, legal, medical, or other professional advice. If authoritative advice is needed, the reader should seek the counsel of a competent professional.

Copyright © 2025 Jonathan Musvosvi
Copyright © 2025 TEACH Services, Inc.
Published in Calhoun, Georgia, USA
ISBN-13: 978-1-4796-1890-3 (Paperback)
ISBN-13: 978-1-4796-1891-0 (ePub)
Library of Congress Control Number: 2025917981

All scripture quotations, unless otherwise indicated, are taken from the New King James Version®. Copyright © 1982 by Thomas Nelson. Used by permission. All rights reserved.

Scripture quotations marked NIV are taken from The Holy Bible, New International Version®, NIV® Copyright ©1973, 1978, 1984, 2011 by Biblica, Inc.® Used by permission. All rights reserved worldwide.

Artwork was generated using artificial intelligence technology with substantial human creative direction and subsequent refinement.

If you wish to contact the author, please use this link to send him an email: 1ref.us/re9457260

Published by

Dedication

I joyfully share the messages in this collection of poetry and dedicate them to God's glory.

Table of Contents

Foreword ix	I Fall to Rise Again.......... 40
Preface 11	It Shall Be Well 41
One Day to Live 13	Faith That Moves Mountains . 42
Interlude: Learning to Forgive; Learning to Heal 14	On the Mountain 43
Let Me Forgive 16	I Shall Not Live in Vain 44
Second Chance.............. 17	The Place of Healing 45
Gifts That Last.............. 18	Interlude: The Master Mender 46
I Shall Love You Again....... 19	Broken 47
Healing Grace 20	Leaving the Past 48
Footprints 21	I'll Seek You Early........... 49
My Heart 22	Out of the Depths........... 50
Longing 23	Deliverance 51
Morning Walk to the River... 24	A Second Life 52
Winds of Care............... 25	Today 53
Quiet Moments............. 26	More Than a Feeling 54
Cover Me................... 27	Built on Sand................ 55
The Wind of Change 28	True Happiness.............. 56
Innocence 29	Bathroom Prayer 57
Nothing Can Stop the Sun ... 30	Guarding the Thoughts 58
Till the Storm Is Done 31	Interlude: A Light to Lead the Way 59
The Scars I Bear 32	The Ancient Path 60
Forgiven................... 33	Interlude: Lifted from the Depths................ 61
All Is Well 34	The Therapist............... 62
Interlude: God's Perfect Forgetfulness 35	A Plea for Mercy............. 63
Releasing the Past........... 36	Interlude: A Many-Colored Message of Grace........ 64
Aging Gracefully............ 37	The Welcome Sign 65
Accepting Who I Am......... 38	Fruitless Day 66
Standing Tall 39	

Interlude: An Absent Lord?..... 67	Christ Within 101
Courage 68	The Exit Door 102
Facing Mountains............ 69	Climb Your Mountain 103
Omissions 70	My Little Cares 104
Forgiven Much 71	After the Storm............. 105
Interlude: The Fatal Dispute 72	My Heart's Temple 106
I Have Forgotten.............. 74	Letting Go 107
Interlude: Mountain Poems 75	I Will Be There 108
The Call of the Hills 76	Fill My Emptiness............ 109
The Peace of the Mountain 77	My Heart Is Like a Fortress.... 110
Hills to Climb 78	The Windows of Your Heart... 111
Interlude: On the Shores of Galilee................. 79	Like the Rose................ 112
	New Beginning.............. 113
A Dream 81	Confidence 114
Emotional Healing............ 82	Let Me Live Beautifully 115
Raining...................... 83	Building Bridges............. 116
Interlude: Walter's Miracle Kidney................. 84	Building Again 117
	The Light of Yesterday 118
The Storm Won't Touch My Heart 86	When I Get Home at Eventide. . 119
	The World Needs You 120
In the Morning 87	X-Ray Eyes.................. 121
Living Waters 88	I Stand So Tall............... 122
Nature's Healing 89	The Setting Sun.............. 123
It Doesn't Pay 90	It Takes So Little 124
Conversion 91	Healing Light 125
The Way I Feel................ 92	Interlude: East from West 126
It's Morning on the Other Side.. 93	Friend of Sinners 128
Provision 94	Turning to the Light.......... 129
Be Still 95	If Jesus Came to Visit.......... 130
Interlude: Where Is Thy Victory? 96	Stay Close to Me............. 131
	I Need You.................. 132
Facing the Night.............. 97	Words You Speak 133
Interlude: Shall We Live Again? . 98	A Letter to My Unborn Child.. 134
Beyond the Setting Sun 99	Bibliography ....
No Winter's Chilling Breeze ... 100	

Foreword

If medicine can heal physical sickness, there is a certain type of poem—just like a spiritual hymn—that can provide emotional healing. Jonathan's poems fall into this category.

It was in 1980 that I first met him. He was my student when I taught history at Solusi College in Zimbabwe. Already at that time, he wrote poetry. I was quite impressed by his poems' unusual depth of thought and insight into the human mind. Just a few years later in 1984, when I worked as an editorial consultant, I had the privilege of publishing Jonathan's first little booklet of poetry.

Jonathan became Dr. Musvosvi, an accomplished university chaplain and lecturer; a pastor and church administrator; but he also continued to write poems. His work gained maturity and empathy, with a special emphasis on forgiveness, emotional healing, and inner peace. Jonathan's poems reveal his deep friendship with Jesus. His words inspire me, and I pray they inspire you.

Dr. Gerhard Padderatz

Preface

At the age of nine, barely able to read and write, I conceived of a dream. I would write messages on small pieces of paper, urging fellow students to surrender their lives to God. I would then nail these notes to trees along the road to school, hoping they would inspire others to seek a deeper connection with God.

Thus, with a pair of scissors, I shredded my exercise book into small pieces of paper. Pencil in hand, l began painstakingly writing the same message on each slip in my native Shona language. The words read, *Ipa moyo wako kuna Jeso. Nekuti kuna Mwari ndicho chinhu* (roughly translated, this means, "Give your heart to Jesus, because in God you find true meaning"). The process was slow and tedious, fitting for a second grader. I felt an immense sense of joy and accomplishment when I finished my first set of notes.

But before I even had a chance to go out and nail my messages to those trees, one of the papers slipped from my pocket. Omega, a playmate, picked it up and read it aloud to a group of students. He was making fun of me.

"Who wrote this?" the others asked.

"It was Jonathan," Omega answered.

Suddenly a voice whispered in my ear, "What will your friends think? Isn't this a bit crazy?" Overcome with embarrassment, I quickly disowned my work. "I didn't write it," I said. "I know nothing about it." And so, my first writing project came to an abrupt, inglorious end.

Fast forward six decades. As I embarked on the journey of writing *The Touch of Grace*, I reflected on that childhood experience. Those simple lines, written with such sincerity, had been etched upon my mind. They were my poetry in its embryonic form. I realized then that God had planted the seed of this gift in me from a very young age.

He placed a longing in my heart to share His message of love through words.

English is my second language, and I sometimes struggle to express myself fluently, but I am grateful for the way God has cultivated this gift over the years. I also wish to thank Judith, my wife of more than forty years. She has been the sounding board for my poetry and played a critical role in the publication of this book. Furthermore, I thank Dr. Gerhard Padderatz for helping me publish my first booklet of poems, *Gift of Love*, in 1984; R. E. Kacelenga for first introducing me to poetry in my first year of high school; Grace Lupepe, who greatly influenced me to like poetry when she taught high school literature; and Allan Phillips, who taught a course in literary criticism which sharpened my writing skills. I also owe a debt of gratitude to my alma maters, Solusi University and Andrews University, for nurturing my gifts.

Finally, I wish to thank all those who allowed me to use their stories in this book. I have altered their names to protect their privacy.

One Day to Live

If I had just one day to live,
One day and nothing more,
If God decreed, "Your time is up,
Just one more day in store."

How would I spend that day with you,
Knowing it was our last?
I'd not waste precious fleeting hours
Reliving conflicts past.

I'd hold you close, each moment dear,
Creating memories.
I'd hope you'd always think of me
With smiles and tender ease.

I'd beg forgiveness for the words
That brought you bitter tears.
I'd try to be the spouse you dreamed
And loved through all these years.

But life is delicate and frail,
Like petals of a flower.
We seldom get a hint or clue
That it's our final hour.

So, love, let us regard each day
As though it were our last.
We may not get that second chance
To mend what's in our past.

Sometimes you will never know the value of a moment until it becomes a memory.
–Theodor Seuss Geisel

Interlude: Learning to Forgive; Learning to Heal

M.C.'S STORY, NARRATED BY THE AUTHOR.

My world fell apart the moment cold hands grabbed my throat. Before I could scream, a sharp knife pressed against my throat.

"Quiet! I'll kill you if you scream."

I was just a boy of sixteen. The man towered over me, more than six feet tall. I was too small, too scared to fight back. My body trembled as he dragged me into an abandoned building by the road.

"Please don't hurt me," I pleaded, my voice shaking.

The man threw me down and forced himself onto me. The gory details are better left unsaid. Afterward, he disappeared.

I lay there motionless, my body bruised and my soul shattered. I had been violated by another man. Everything I knew about myself—my worth, my innocence—crumbled. Eventually, I forced myself to rise up, but something inside me felt irreparably broken. I walked home, tears streaming down my face.

In the months that followed, I couldn't sleep. Every night the nightmares came: his face, his hands, the helplessness. Anger took root in me. I turned to marijuana, hoping it might numb the pain, but it only deepened my darkness.

Six years later, my life was in ruins. I ended up in a treatment center for drug addiction. It was there that my therapist gently unravelled the thread that led back to the assault. My stress, my depression, my substance abuse; they all stemmed from that day.

One day my therapist asked me, "Can you forgive him?"

I froze. "I can't. I hate him." My voice trembled with rage. "He violated me."

"Ask God to help you forgive," he suggested quietly.

I was desperate. I was broken. I hadn't realized how deeply unforgiveness had poisoned my life. And maybe—just maybe—there was a chance for healing if I tried. So I prayed, "God, I'm sorry for hating this man. Help me forgive."

As the words left my mouth, something shifted inside me. It wasn't immediate, but a burden I had carried for years started to lift. I felt a peace I hadn't known since the assault. The anger and hate, though not entirely gone, began to dissolve. It was the beginning of my healing. Eventually I quit drugs, and step by step I reclaimed my life. Years later I found myself standing before a congregation preaching about forgiveness; something I had once thought impossible.

> *Maybe—just maybe—there was a chance for healing if I tried.*

When I look back on that awful day, I no longer feel the hatred that once consumed me. Instead, I feel pity for the man. He doesn't know Christ. He doesn't know the freedom that comes from forgiveness. I pray for him that he might find grace, as I did.

Let Me Forgive

Let me forgive with my whole mind
Despite the pain I feel,
For if I do not let it go,
These scars may never heal.

The past will chain me like a slave,
And I'll remain oppressed.
I break my chains when I forgive
And lay the past to rest.

Let me forgive with all my heart;
If I do not forgive,
You'll hurt my feelings and my thoughts
And I'll be your captive.

Forgiveness breaks your fierce control
Over the way I feel.
Your hold on me I now release,
The surest way to heal.

Forgiveness grants me wings to soar,
Like a caged bird set free.
O God, lift me on eagle wings;
From vengeance let me flee.

Bearing with one another, and forgiving one another, if anyone has a complaint against another; even as Christ forgave you, so you also must do.
–Colossians 3:13

Second Chance

Last night I dreamed I visited
The land called Second Chance,
Where broken lives were made anew
And freed from past offense.

Its gates of mercy opened wide
And welcomed me to stay.
Could I, who once had cursed its Prince
Be welcomed on this day?

The New Beginning river flowed,
Its waters crystal clear.
Shedding my dark despair and doubt,
I plunged without a fear.

My weary soul found sweet release
Deep in that sacred stream.
Delivered, I embraced new dawn
And woke up from my dream.

*Therefore, if anyone is in Christ, he is a new creation;
old things have passed away; behold,
all things have become new.*
–2 Corinthians 5:17

Gifts That Last

God, make me rich in things that matter.
I may not own a bank account
Or grand estates to awe my neighbor,
But make me rich in ways that count.

Make me abundant in my kindness,
For there are lonely souls in grief.
Perhaps my presence in their valley
Could bring a season of relief.

Let me be generous with friendship;
So many crave the human touch.
The old who live in isolation
May feel uplifted by my reach.

Though I have little cash to offer,
Fill me with boundless empathy.
These are the gifts that last forever,
And I can share them endlessly.

---

*Too often we underestimate the power of a touch, a smile,
a kind word, a listening ear, an honest compliment,
or the smallest act of caring, all of which have
the potential to turn a life around.*
–Leo Buscaglia

I Shall Love You Again

When life's brief day has reached its final close
And night has drawn me in,
Grieve for a time but not for very long;
Let healing soon begin.

Remember death is but a fleeting sleep—
Reunion waits ahead.
The old forgotten graves will open wide
When saints rise from the dead.

When you miss me, don't mark anniversaries
To save your soul from pain.
Seek solace in the promises we hold—
You'll find peace once again.

When you miss me, reflect on your own life
And do not live in vain.
Prepare to meet me on reunion day—
I shall love you again.

For the Lord Himself will descend from heaven with a shout, with the voice of an archangel, and with the trumpet of God. And the dead in Christ will rise first.
–1 Thessalonians 4:16

Healing Grace

O God, Your healing grace
Is what I seek today.
There's no disease or pain
Your touch can't soothe away.

I come just as I am,
Worn down and scarred by sin.
O God of mercy, mend
The brokenness within.

Reverse the moral rot,
My conscience cleanse anew,
Lead me back to the paths
Of innocence I knew.

Your X-ray eyes can see
What shame I seek to hide.
With gentle grace, Lord, fill
The aching void inside.

O Lord, refine my ways,
So friends or foes may see
The likeness of Your Son
Displayed so clear in me.

*And He said to me, "My grace is sufficient for you,
for my strength is made perfect in weakness."
–2 Corinthians 12:9*

Footprints

I'll leave deep footprints on the trail
That I am walking through
So those who follow in my steps
Will find the path I knew.

My children's eyes look up to me;
I'm like their guiding light.
Long after I am gone, I hope
They'll follow with delight.

I'll carve my footprints bold and deep,
Footprints to mark the way,
So those seeking the way to life
Won't stumble in dismay.

Footprints engraved with deepest care
For loved ones left behind—
May these bold prints through countless years
Stay etched upon their minds.

My Heart

My heart is such a fragile thing,
So handle with great care.
It cradles feelings deep inside,
Emotions sweet and rare.

A careless word can steal its joy—
So delicate and frail—
Show not a cold, disdainful gaze
Lest tenderness should pale.

My heart, though built to love and trust,
Needs soft ways like a dove.
It needs the touch of gentle hands;
In warmth, it nurtures love.

My heart was made to foster love—
Hate poisons its sweet springs—
I cherish every beat and pulse
And all the joys it brings.

*Keep your heart with all diligence,
for out of it spring the issues of life.
–Proverbs 4:23*

Longing

I'm longing for Your coming, Lord,
As wilting cornfields crave for rain.
You've been absent for far too long—
Come quickly, Lord, or life feels vain.

Come as You did to Bethlehem;
I'll make a room within my heart.
Is that You knocking at my door?
Come in and never more depart.

Dwell in the depth of my cold heart
And warm it with Your tenderness.
It's hardened like a block of ice—
Melt down all greed and selfishness.

Come like sweet sunrise in my heart
When all my world is dark and drear.
Come even so, Lord Jesus, come …
The knocking at my door I hear.

Jesus answered and said to him, "If anyone loves Me, he will keep My word: and My Father will love him, and We will come to him and make Our home with him."
–John 14:23

Morning Walk to the River

Today I walked down to the river
To spend quiet moments there,
For in the street where crowds are roaming
My soul shriveled with care.

"I went to seek the Savior's presence!"
A voice within me cried.
I yearned for peace and clear direction,
With Him alone as guide.

The river's calm embraced my spirit
Where water lilies bloomed,
Where weaver birds with chirping voices
Sang joy into my gloom.

I felt my heavy burdens lifted;
The skies were vivid blue.
I left the river's peaceful waters
Revived, refreshed, and new.

> Come to Me, all you who labor and are heavy laden, and I will give you rest.
> –Matthew 11:28

Winds of Care

Today the winds are wild and strong—
My heart is yearning for sweet rest—
Down to the river I must go
To ease the turmoil in my breast.

Last time I lingered by its banks
I found God's peace awaiting there.
Beside still waters we conversed;
His peace dispelled my deep despair.

Today, my soul is drawn once more
To that serene, calm riverside.
Though winds oppose, I'll find my way.
I shall return with peace inside.

Quiet Moments

I draw a lot of strength from silence,
So in the morning I retreat
Into a very quiet corner
Where only God and I can meet.

And during quiet meditation,
God visits me just like a friend.
He comes with healing grace upon me
And gives me peace the world can't find.

I rise from there rejuvenated,
Equipped to face a thousand foes.
I rise with strength to scale high mountains,
Eager to do the Master's chores.

… In quietness and confidence shall be your strength.
–Isaiah 30:15

Cover Me

God, cover me with righteousness
As snow enshrouds the sullied ground.
Let me stand pure before Your eyes—
Cleanse me and turn my life around.

Erase dark shadows of my past,
Let them lie covered by Your blood.
You see the mire where I am trapped—
Rescue and draw me from the mud.

Cover me like a pure white robe,
Let grace conceal my past misdeeds.
You know the darkest fears I hold—
Grant me the peace my spirit needs.

Cover my past beneath your blood
And cleanse the dark blot deep inside.
God, grant that I might stand and say,
"I have no more secrets to hide."

"Come now, and let us reason together," says the Lord. "Though your sins are like scarlet, they shall be as white as snow; though they are red like crimson, they shall be as wool."
–Isaiah 1:18

The Wind of Change

God, send a strong wind sweeping through my heart,
A wind of change from You.
Blow out the dust that settled in my soul
And let clean air flow through.

God, let Your wind dispel the web of sin
Which time allowed to grow.
Cleanse me anew with Your great Spirit's touch,
Let pure thoughts overflow.

God, let Your mighty Spirit blow through me,
Bring forth the latter rain,
Send the refreshment that I crave so deep—
Revive my soul again.

> *Be glad then, you children of Zion, and rejoice in the Lord your God; for He has given you the former rain faithfully, and He will cause the rain to come down to you—the former rain, and the latter rain ….*
> –Joel 2:23

Innocence

Grant me the heart I used to hold
When I was young and mild.
Before I soiled my soul with sin,
My dreams were undefiled.

Once, laughter filled my days with cheer—
No hatred marred my stay—
I felt a kinship with all those
Who chanced upon my way.

My motives were clear like daylight
Before pride took control—
Now things are different; selfish greed
Has fouled my once-pure soul.

The grown-up man knows only strife:
We stampede for our share;
We clash for status, power, and fame,
And mar our days with care.

O how I long to turn back time
And mend the broken trust.
I yearn for my lost innocence—
A soul once pure and just.

> *... Unless you are converted
> and become as little children,
> you will by no means enter the kingdom of heaven.*
> –Matthew 18:3

Nothing Can Stop the Sun

No power can stop the sun from rising,
Though skies look dark and bleak.
This night is but a fleeting season—
The morning will soon break.

Say not the world is total darkness,
For half the globe is light.
I'm dwelling on the side that's shining—
One side is always bright.

No force can block the sun from shining
Though clouds may veil its face.
Behind them lies a silver lining—
The sun shines in its place.

God's sun will break this grip of winter,
Its rays will melt the cold.
Spring will arrive with warmth and beauty
When nature's blooms unfold.

Nothing can mute my heart's sweet singing,
Even when grief is near.
My heart sings songs of faith and courage—
All sorrows disappear.

> *Through the Lord's mercies we are not consumed, because His compassions fail not. They are new every morning; great is Your faithfulness.*
> *–Lamentations 3:22, 23*

Till the Storm Is Done

When rain keeps pounding from the sky
And slows your progress down,
When you are groping in despair,
Wait till the storm is done.

Look for a very quiet spot
And pause there for a while.
God knows we need forced rest sometimes,
So greet it with a smile.

No storm can rage forever, friend;
Watch for the rainbow sign.
God always makes the storm to pass
And brings the perfect shine.

The sun will warm your face again
Once clouds have drifted past.
Wait patiently and shed no tear—
The weather will not last.

> ... Weeping may endure for a night,
> but joy comes in the morning.
> –Psalm 30:5

The Scars I Bear

The scars I carry deep inside
Made me a stronger man.
Though Satan sought my swift demise,
God crafted His own plan.

The scars reveal my broken past—
My flaws were laid so bare—
But healing grace has mended me;
These marks reveal God's care.

My scars remind me I survived
Sin's sharp and cruel knife.
I'm on the road to wholeness now,
God healed and save my life.

> "For I will restore health to you and heal you of your wounds," says the Lord.
> –Jeremiah 30:17

Forgiven

Because You have forgiven me,
I bear my sin no more.
I stand unblemished, just like Christ,
Who never sinned before.

You harbor no hard feelings, God,
For You chose to forget.
In Your forgiveness I stand tall,
Though I'm not perfect yet.

If unforgiveness stains my heart,
I lay it at Your feet.
Remind me of the cross You bore
To cover my deceit.

Make me a beacon of Your grace
To those who cross my way.
Let conflict cease and peace increase,
Let grace and love hold sway.

*As far as the east is from the west, so far has
He removed our transgressions from us.*
–Psalm 103:12

All Is Well

Lord, it's so comforting that all is well
Between my soul and You.
You hold no grudge against me, though You know
My sin that sticks like glue.

You forgave sins I can't forgive myself
And filled my heart with peace.
You forgot things that I still can't forget
And gave me sweet release.

Thank you for granting me a clean new life
Without a spot of blame.
Remember me when You return to earth—
In Your book write my name.

Interlude: God's Perfect Forgetfulness

I treasure Bible verses that speak of God's forgetfulness. I've marked and underlined these passages to remind me that God chooses to forget my sinful acts.

His forgetfulness isn't due to memory lapses. God's memory is perfect; nothing is hidden from His eyes (Heb. 4:13). Yet He chooses to forget every sin you confess; He doesn't hold grudges. As Micah 7:19 says, "You will cast all our sins into the depths of the sea." They are completely out of His sight. Isaiah 38:17 echoes this: "For You have cast all my sins behind Your back." God never turns to look at them again.

However, Satan keeps an accurate record of every sin he has tempted us to commit. He constantly reminds us of our transgressions, hoping to lead us to despair.

Despite God's promises, I confess that I often dwell on past mistakes. It's human to look back, but once you confess your sins, "He is faithful and just to forgive us our sins and to cleanse us from all unrighteousness" (1 John 1:9). God reassures us in Jeremiah 31:34, "For I will forgive their iniquity, and their sin I will remember no more."

When you recall your sinful deeds, recite one of God's many promises of forgiveness. Why rack your soul with guilt when God commands, "Do not remember the former things, nor consider the things of old" (Isa. 43:18)?

Releasing the Past

I stand at the threshold of a new dawn;
The night has vanished with my sleep.
God rolled it like a blanket off the earth
As morning rose from shadows deep.

My mind reflects on what I must release—
The past should pass, just like the night.
O God, remove the spirit of revenge
That blights my soul and dims my light.

Help me release these ancient grievances
That linger like a festering sore.
O Grace, now touch and heal my wounded soul
And mend the bond we had before.

Let me move past the petty jealousies,
The feuds that poisoned fellowship.
The journey of our life is brief and swift—
We need each other's partnership.

God, at the start of such a pristine day,
Dispel the shadows from my heart.
Make my life fairer than the morning light
And help me make a brand-new start.

---

*Looking carefully lest anyone fall short of the grace of God;
lest any root of bitterness springing up cause trouble,
and by this many become defiled.*
–Hebrews 12:15

Aging Gracefully

Let me age gracefully, like the setting sun;
I'm near the end of life's brief race.
In my declining years, Lord, draw me near
So I may showcase Your rich grace.

Let me not whine about the aches I feel
That constantly afflict my bones.
It's the new normal that I must accept—
No one delights to hear my moans.

As memory fades, let me also forget
The petty feuds that tore apart.
Why should I nurse a grudge until the grave
And forfeit God's peace in my heart?

As winter years begin, grant me content,
Just give me health and peace of mind.
Make me a good example to the young
Who trace the footprints left behind.

A life well-lived is a testimony to the grace and faithfulness of God.
–Unknown

Accepting Who I Am

Because I accept who I am,
I feel at ease and free.
The limits life has placed on me
No longer trouble me.

I focus on my given strengths:
God granted me a mind;
He set the path that I should walk
To uplift humankind.

I'm not a finished work of art,
I've faults I cannot hide.
It took a hundred years or more
For oaks to soar in pride.

I'm growing slowly to the point
Where God wants me to be.
Each day I mark a milestone grand:
His Spirit sets me free.

I may have come from humble roots,
But that shaped who I am.
I'm changing like a butterfly;
I'll never be the same.

*For we are His workmanship,
created in Christ Jesus for good works ….*
–Ephesians 2:10

Standing Tall

Let me stand tall and straight today,
Much taller than my frame.
A higher purpose, Lord, I seek
Than chasing fleeting fame.

Grant me a heart to serve the poor
Who can't repay my deed.
Purge from my soul with gentle grace
The stain of selfish greed.

Let me not, for rich profit's sake,
Exploit the humble poor.
There's so much fairness I can give
To all who seek my door.

Let me stand tall that I may find
No crooked deal to hide.
Then when my day draws to its end,
I'll close my race with pride.

I Fall to Rise Again

I entertained great dreams that crashed,
I planned and wished in vain;
But though I tripped I'm like the tide—
I fall to rise again.

I dreamed of heights beyond the stars,
Yet tumbled in the drain.
But I'm not whining in the ditch—
Like wind I rise again.

So long as God stands by my side,
I triumph through all pain,
And I resurge like ocean waves—
I fall to rise again.

I've promises I must fulfill,
I've dreams I must attain.
I've set my eyes beyond the stars—
God, help me rise again.

*Our greatest glory is not in never falling,
but in rising every time we fall.*
–Oliver Goldsmith

It Shall Be Well

Today the skies are dark and dreary,
The chilling rain pours down so fast,
But if I just keep on believing,
It shall be well with me at last.

Already I can see the rainbow—
The promise of tranquility—
I shall not stay long in rough weather
Because God will come through for me.

Let me endure just for this moment
The stress and strain inside my heart.
Let me keep calm just like the statue.
It shall be well, this will depart.

Faith That Moves Mountains

I need faith that moves mountains—
I've such a pressing need—
O God, provide quick answers;
My heart's petitions heed.

The way ahead looks crooked,
I know not where to turn.
Let me just pause a moment—
There are lessons I must learn.

I shall stand still in silence
And let God speak to me.
I will seek His direction
In answer to my plea.

His hand that shapes my destiny
Controls the stars above.
God will not doze or slumber
Until the mountains move.

On the Mountain

The bitter thoughts of vengeance
That plagued me through the year—
I shed them on the mountain
Where I met God in prayer.

The sad discord between us,
The spite I could not bear,
Dissolved like mist at sunrise
When God drew ever near.

I lost the hate I harbored—
My heart feels light as air—
So glad I climbed the mountain
And made peace with Him there.

From the end of the earth I will cry to You, when my heart is overwhelmed; lead me to the rock that is higher than I.
–Psalm 61:2

I Shall Not Live in Vain

I shall not live this day in vain;
It dawns upon my world but once.
If great exploits are mine to claim,
This moment holds my finest chance.

The day is swift, these precious hours
Will gallop into history.
Let me relieve a little pain
From man or beast just near to me.

Let me find strength to lift a load—
Some heart will cheer up if I care.
Let me plant roses where I stand
To spread sweet fragrance in the air.

I shall not live this day in vain
Just rocking idly in the chair—
I need a purpose for my life
To spread some joy and show I care.

The Place of Healing

There is a place called Calvary Hill
Where those with stigma from the past
Can find their hearts and spirits healed,
Their broken lives made whole at last.

That place I recommend to you;
The Savior waits with tender care
To heal old scars and make you whole
And lift all shadows of despair.

I often visit Calvary Hill
In seasons of distress and grief.
Old Calvary's just a prayer away;
So near, the hill of kind relief.

Interlude: The Master Mender

Jesus worked as a carpenter in Nazareth before He began His ministry (Mark 6:3). I imagine neighbors bringing broken chairs for Him to fix. Jesus became an expert at repairing broken things, His hands crafting each item with great care. Every item of furniture Jesus repaired revealed His flawless craftsmanship.

After His baptism at about thirty, His role shifted to repairing broken lives and families. Old Nazareth must have had many such broken lives. Nathanael, who knew the depths of its depravity, once remarked, "Can anything good come out of Nazareth?" (John 1:46).

But for Jesus, there seemed to be no better place to begin His salvation work. Wherever He turned He saw an alcoholic, a prostitute, or a demoniac in need of His grace. He announced right there in Nazareth, "The Spirit of the Lord is upon Me, because He has anointed Me to preach the gospel to the poor; He has sent Me to heal the brokenhearted, to proclaim liberty to the captives" (Luke 4:18). Fixing just one broken life often made Jesus' day, and for Him no life was too broken to be fixed.

He frequently went out of His way to seek the wretched. Remember His encounter with Legion? More than 1,000 demons wreaked havoc in one man's life. Yet Jesus sailed on a turbulent sea at night to distant Gadarenes, His eyes having spotted that one maniac in need of healing grace.

Do you feel as if your life is a total wreck? Do you feel you have lost the hope of salvation? Today Jesus is still in the business of fixing the broken. Whatever brokenness you may be experiencing, Jesus can fix it. It is a job He is willing and able to do.

Broken

Great Carpenter of Nazareth,
You fixed the broken chairs.
I'm shattered, Lord, please gather me
From fragments of despair.

God of rich grace, reach down to me;
You know where deep cracks lie.
Who else can mend these faults but You?
To You alone I cry.

My life craves for its Maker's touch
To make the broken whole.
Great Carpenter, restore what's lost
And heal this sin-sick soul.

My heart is worn and weary, Lord,
Beneath the weight of sin.
Great Healer, mend the fractured soul;
Bring calm and peace within.

He heals the brokenhearted and binds up their wounds.
–Psalm 147:3

Leaving the Past

I've closed the door on yesterday,
Accepting what it cost.
I cannot mend its shattered dreams
Or call back time that's lost.

The vain regrets from time long past?
I tossed them all behind,
For Grace touched me and healed my wounds—
I walk with peace of mind.

Don't judge me by my sorrowed past
Or crooked ways you know.
I've laid old history in its grave—
Bygones don't haunt me now.

Last night at Calvary's sacred heights,
Grace banished all despair.
I've found a brand-new way to live
With peace beyond compare.

Forget the former things; do not dwell on the past.
–Isaiah 43:18 (NIV)

I'll Seek You Early

I'll seek You early in the morning
When day has just begun,
And like the songbird I'll awaken
Before the rising sun.

Your mercies fall around each morning
Like dew upon the grass.
I'll rise to pick the morning manna
Before the blessings pass.

I'll seek You when the day is dawning
While earth is still at rest.
I need Your light to shine upon me
And put all doubts to rest.

Out of the Depths

Out of the depths, oh Lord, I call to You;
Please hear my anguished cry.
If You should count each sin against my soul,
How would I stand Your eye?

But there's a tender mercy in Your heart,
Forgiveness full and free.
My eyes look up like flowers to the sun—
Your grace has covered me.

I've calmed and quieted my restless soul
And laid my burdens down.
In Your embrace my heart has found its peace—
Your righteousness, my crown.

King David once prayed, "But you, O Lord,
be merciful to me, and raise me up …."
–Psalm 41:10
His son Solomon said, "For a righteous man
may fall seven times and rise again …."
–Proverbs 24:16

Deliverance

Lord, occupy the chamber of my heart
Where greed has laid its claim.
Illuminate the darkness, seize control,
And quench this burning flame.

Remind me of my mortal fleeting state—
This breath that cannot last—
And though I may own mansions in my day,
Soon dust returns to dust.

I cannot take gold into mouldy graves,
The tombs are destitute;
So help me seek eternal treasures now—
From greed, Lord, liberate.

> For what will it profit a man if he gains the whole world,
> and loses his own soul?
> –Mark 8:36

A Second Life

Life is too sacred to be spent in vain
And snatched by cruel death.
In seventy years, we glimpse but just a part
Of God's will for our birth.

Death and the grave, they were not God's design;
He never willed our pain.
A second life must heal our broken earth
And end the reign of sin.

God will make all things new on planet Earth;
The grave shall be no more.
Ten billion years shall feel like our first day
On heaven's golden shore.

Today

As I draw back the curtains
And gaze towards the light,
I see the new day dawning
With dreams within my sight.

Let me embrace this moment
And fling the past behind;
I'll break the old addictions
That long have chained my mind.

Though yesterday I stumbled
And stained my soul with mud,
I see new life before me
Unfolding like a bud.

With God to shape my destiny
And faith to guide my way,
My future glows with promise—
Thank God I lived today.

Nurture your mind with great thoughts.
To believe in the heroic makes heroes.
–Benjamin Disraeli, *Coningsby*

More Than a Feeling

Love is more than a feeling
Inside the tender heart,
For feelings change like weather—
The bright days may depart.

Love is defined by reason;
Her eyes are not so blind.
Love kindles deep devotion
And keeps us sweet and kind.

Love is a firm conviction
Anchored in principle:
With steady aim and focus,
Like needle to the pole.

Since I stood at the altar
To pledge my hand to you,
I've not moved one step backwards.
I've been steadfast and true.

Built on Sand

Love that is based on outer charm
Is like a mansion built on sand.
It lacks the strength to face life's storms;
Its weak foundation cannot stand.

Love based on riches or great fame
Is like a bird with broken wings.
It cannot rise, remains earthbound,
For love can't thrive on fleeting things.

Love springing from your selfish greed
Is poisoned dinner from the start.
It seeks to please itself alone;
At last, it breaks the tender heart.

Go look for virtue in the heart
And you'll find love sincere and true.
Seek for rich gold in character—
Then joy and peace will camp near you.

True Happiness

True happiness springs from within,
You need not wander far.
You chase a fleeting shadow, friend—
It blooms right where you are.

Look deep inside your restless heart;
If barren, plant a seed.
Let kindness blossom like the rose
And fill some human need.

Let deeds of mercy fill your heart,
Be gracious, kind, and true—
Then happiness like dawn's soft light
Will rise and shine on you.

Bathroom Prayer

As I turn on the shower taps
To wash the filth away,
I think of deeper stains within:
The sins that marred my day.

Though water rinses dirt away,
It can't cleanse hidden sin.
Your grace alone can purify
The dark desires within.

The guilt that haunts my sinful soul
Yearns for Your healing touch.
O God, wash me so pure and white
And free me from sin's clutch.

Let Your sweet Spirit fill my soul,
My body, and my mind.
Refine my nature, shape my heart,
To what You long designed.

---

*Wash me thoroughly from my iniquity,
and cleanse me from my sin.*
—Psalm 51:2

Guarding the Thoughts

I shall guard thoughts I entertain;
The mind shall not roam wild and free.
I'm shaped by thoughts I plant inside,
For as a man thinks, so is he.

Thoughts are the compass of my soul:
They guide the vessel through the gale.
Thoughts are like wings upon my back:
Lifting me high, I shall not fail.

I shall inspire and cleanse my thoughts
With words straight from the Holy Book.
I shall focus on lofty dreams
And seek a positive outlook.

I shall recite a sacred psalm
To draw me closer to my Lord;
I'll dwell on themes that elevate
And walk with Him the higher road.

Interlude: A Light to Lead the Way

My mother had only one year of formal schooling. When she left school, she was barely literate. However, driven by her deep desire to study the Scriptures, she taught herself to read. Though she passed away more than thirty years ago, I still hold fond memories of her sitting under the shade of a tree, quietly reading her Bible. And I recall her softly asking me when I returned home at sunset from tending cattle, "Did you remember to visit your secret prayer spot in the bush?"

That simple question embodied the deep faith she instilled in me and my seven siblings. Through her unwavering devotion, we were given a rich Christian heritage that continues to guide us today.

The Ancient Path

This is the path my mother's feet once sought.
At dawn she'd steal away;
She'd seek solace beside a flowing stream
And let her worries stray.

She rose as cattle lowed in misty pens,
While shepherds slept in dreams.
She trod this ancient trail with sacred tunes
Beside the murmuring streams.

This is the path she chose when her heart yearned
For sacred, quiet space:
A place to cast aside domestic cares
And find relief in grace.

Now grass has overgrown this well-worn trail;
She walks this path no more.
O, how my heart longs to revive the path
My mother walked before.

Interlude: Lifted from the Depths

Otieno walked into my office on a Monday morning. His eyes were bloodshot as he pleaded for help. "For the last few months," he said, "I've been drinking as soon as I get up in the morning. I can't control the amount I drink or the frequency." He moaned, "My life is totally ruined. Just yesterday, my wife deserted me. "About a month ago," he explained, "I started hallucinating after drinking. That scared my wife because my father died of alcoholism. Before he died, he suffered from hallucinations." Otieno then burst into tears.

"Are you serious about wanting to quit?" I asked him.

"I really want to, but I'm a slave to it. I have tried a dozen times and failed."

He had tried in vain to fight the addiction by relying on his willpower. I quoted the promise of Jesus to him: "So if the Son sets you free, you will be free indeed" (John 8:36, NIV). We began studying the Scriptures and praying together. I introduced him to Jesus, who came to "destroy the works of the devil" (1 John 3:8).

Over the next few months, I witnessed a heroic fight. "This is a life-or-death matter to me," Otieno once cried. I saw how human effort combined with Christ's strength enable an alcoholic to conquer addiction. He relapsed a couple of times, but each time he quickly confessed his sin and recommitted his life to God.

One day he called me to his office, where he showed me a pack of cigarettes.

"Who do they belong to?" I asked.

"I've been a heavy smoker since my high school days, but I haven't smoked one cigarette for weeks now," he said with a broad smile. Apparently, giving up alcohol was helping him to clean up other areas of his life, too.

What a thrill it was to see Otieno getting a new shot at life. His self-confidence and self-esteem increased, and his wife came back. "Thank God for this rebirth," she celebrated.

One day Otieno asked me, "What can stop me from getting baptized?"

I looked at him with a smile and responded, "Nothing." Christ the bondage-breaker had set him free.

The Therapist

I know the good kind Therapist
Who mends each broken heart.
He'll stitch the pieces though your life
Seems torn and falls apart.

My life was once a hopeless dream;
Despair had gripped my soul.
But then this gentle Therapist
Restored and made me whole.

He'll do the same for you, my friend;
His heart feels all your pain.
With grace so boundless and profound,
He'll make you whole again.

But where sin abounded, grace abounded much more.
–Romans 5:20

A Plea for Mercy

Deal gently with Your wayward servant—
My heart is filled with dread—
I fear I may lose my salvation,
Though ransom price is paid.

When I look straight into the mirror,
So many faults I see.
I fall short of Your perfect standard;
Sin still clings on to me.

Lord, turn my gaze from self to Calvary,
Show me the crimson flood.
You said there's no more condemnation
If I'm under Your blood.

Your blood is my eternal refuge;
My fears are swept away.
I'm sheltered by Your boundless mercy—
I feel assured today.

We should not make self the center and indulge anxiety and fear as to whether we shall be saved. All this turns the soul away from the Source of our strength. Commit the keeping of your soul to God and trust in Him.
–Ellen White

Interlude: A Many-Colored Message of Grace

God encircled His throne with a rainbow. This arc is a symbol of His mercy. He first revealed the rainbow as a sign of His covenant with planet Earth just after His fierce judgement with the flood. The catastrophe was universal. Lest sinful human beings should live in constant fear of His wrath, God made a solemn commitment:

"Thus I establish My covenant with you: Never again shall all flesh be cut off by the waters of the flood: never again shall there be a flood to destroy the earth." And God said, "This is the sign of the covenant which I make between Me and you …. I set My rainbow in the cloud, and it shall be for the sign of the covenant between Me and the earth." (Gen. 9:11-13)

Isn't it amazing that God chose to surround His throne with this great symbol of mercy, first revealed to Noah? Isn't He communicating to us that He deals with us from the mercy seat? Thank you, God, for the everlasting sign of mercy encircling Your throne.

The Welcome Sign

Thank You, God, for the rainbow by Your throne;
Today it strengthened me.
How kind of You to spread that sign of grace
For errant souls to see.

I almost drew back, feeling quite unfit
To stand before Your face,
But then You wrote in purple, blue, and red,
You're welcome to this place.

Thank You for grace that covers all my sin—
The answer to my plea—
You circled Your throne with this mercy sign
For timid guests like me.

*… And there was a rainbow around the throne,
in appearance like an emerald.*
–Revelation 4:3

Fruitless Day

As I look back across my day
And count the deeds I've done,
I find no thoughtful, caring acts
To help upraise someone.

I might have hugged the weeping child
To soothe his silent tears,
And banished from his world the cold
That chilled his tender years.

I was the angel sent by Grace
To mend a broken heart,
To give the tender human touch
When life seemed all apart.

But then I slammed my heart's door shut
And strove for selfish gain.
I made my fortune, yet I sense
I lived this day in vain.

Interlude: An Absent Lord?

Just after the French Revolution, Thomas Paine disseminated new ideas about God. He believed in the existence of one God, but he speculated that after God created the universe, He just abandoned it to run on its own, like a clock. This philosophy of religion is called deism. Paine taught that God simply established the laws of science to govern the operation of the universe. He isn't intimately involved in its affairs; He's detached like an absent lord.

If that's all true, our groaning won't touch His heart. It's futile to cry to Him. We're on our own. And when I reflect on my Christian journey, I confess that often times I lived like a deist. I related to God as though He were totally indifferent to my needs. Now, don't get me wrong. Theologically, I never subscribed to deism. I always knew that the Scriptures teach about a compassionate, loving God, but I gave only mental assent to the doctrine.

As a teenager and a young adult, I had no space for God in my life. I battled life's challenges on my own, just like a deist (for example, I suffered much from psychosomatic illness). To be honest, God became the absent Lord in my life. I knew God existed, but I seldom sought Him. I seldom read His Word or consulted Him. I made life's choices without reference to Him. How, then, could He gain relevance?

Then, I missed the peace that comes from knowing that I have a Savior close by my side, Someone in charge of my eternal destiny. I thank God that I now know that I have a Father who watches over me. He cares about every detail in my life as though I was His only child on earth. He tells me, "The very hairs of your head are all numbered" (Matt. 10:30). With such a God watching over me, I can cast all my cares upon Him.

Courage

I need not feel so downcast;
I'll wait upon the Lord.
He knows the way to lighten
What weighs me down so hard.

His hand directs the planets
As they spin through the skies;
No star strays from its orbit,
Held firm by His designs.

God never blinks one moment
In His eternal reign,
Or chaos would grip the planets
And life be lost in vain.

Why should I feel so anxious?
His strength will see me through.
He'll lift me on His shoulder
When skies turn black or blue.

Why are you cast down, O my soul? And why are you disquieted within me? Hope in God; for I shall yet praise Him, the help of my countenance and my God.
—Psalm 43:5

Facing Mountains

As I look back across the miles
I've traveled since my birth,
I see a strong, unfailing Hand
That shaped my being and worth.

I see the rough, steep hills behind
That I once feared to climb;
But strength to scale those rugged peaks
Arrived in perfect time.

At each sheer precipice I found
New strength to help me cope.
My Guide's hand kept my spirit strong
As I climbed up each slope.

And so today why should I fear
The daunting path ahead?
One day I'll turn and gladly say,
"It was God's hand that led."

Omissions

It's not some gruesome, grisly crime,
But small things left undone
That rob my conscience of its peace
When my long day is done.

The sick old man I did not call
Until it was too late,
The humble word of my regret
I felt too proud to state,

The beggar's plea I brushed aside,
The debt I left unpaid,
The word of faith I did not share,
The prayer I left unsaid—

These are the things that haunt my dreams
And fleece my soul of peace.
Oh no, it's not some grisly crime
That robs life of its ease.

Forgiven Much

Because I've been forgiven much,
God, soften up my heart of stone;
Put tender feelings in my breast
And shut the door to hate and scorn.

Forgiveness is not mine to hoard;
Forgiveness flows through me to share.
Forgiveness heals each bleeding sore—
God, give me grace to love and care.

Because I've been forgiven much,
This bitterness can have no room.
I choose to love and trust again
And lay old grudges in the tomb.

For if you forgive men their trespasses, your heavenly Father will also forgive you.
–Matthew 6:14

Interlude: The Fatal Dispute

A parable

Robert and Nellie lived under the same roof for two long years without exchanging a single word. Neither was willing to break the silence with the first word of apology.

Their marriage, once filled with romance and joy, had soured in the course of one night. A single argument had unraveled it all. The quarrel erupted over the growing expenses required to care for Nellie's ailing mother. Tragically, the dispute occurred within earshot of the very person they were arguing about. That same night Nellie's mother's blood pressure spiked, and she was rushed to the hospital. She died the next day.

Grief-stricken, Nellie couldn't shake the belief that the argument had triggered her mother's sudden death. Her heart flooded with anguish, and in a moment of blind pain she accused Robert, "You killed my mother."

Robert, equally devastated, lashed back, "You started the quarrel, not me."

From that moment, neither could forgive the other. Hurt and resentment ran deep, solidifying their icy silence. Both were prisoners of their pride, and their marriage eventually crumbled into a bitter divorce.

Their story echoes the haunting truth expressed by Roberto Assagioli: "Without forgiveness, life is governed by an endless cycle of resentment and retaliation." But why is forgiveness so difficult for so many? Why do we hesitate to humble ourselves and ask for mercy, or extend it when we've been wronged?

I've come to realize that when Christ dwells in my heart, forgiveness becomes possible—even when it seems impossible. Yielding to His counsel, as expressed through the Apostle Paul, makes it easier to let go of the pain: "Be kind to one another, tenderhearted, forgiving one another, even as God in Christ forgave you" (Eph. 4:32).

In the end, unforgiveness builds walls that trap us in bitterness and rob us of peace. If only we could remember: life is too short to live imprisoned by resentment. Only when we allow love to tear down those walls can we experience the healing power of grace. True freedom is found in forgiveness, and that freedom is a gift we all deserve to give and receive.

> *Unforgiveness builds walls that trap us in bitterness and rob us of peace.*

I Have Forgotten

I have forgotten spiteful words
We traded yesterday;
The poison thoughts I nursed so long
Dissolved like mist away.

A rainbow arched through stormy skies—
God's sign of peace with foes—
Then I released the hurt I bore,
The old, unsettled woes.

I trust you too erased the past—
The memories of our feud—
And though my words stung like a bee,
I pray the pain has healed.

As night descends and calm prevails,
As deeds pass in review,
Let sleep bestow forgetfulness
And guide us to renew.

I set My rainbow in the cloud, and it shall be for the sign of the covenant between Me and the earth.
–Genesis 9:13

Interlude: Mountain Poems

I have been in love with mountains from my childhood days. I grew up on our family farm right at the foot of a mountain. As a youth, I often climbed the mountain just to get that feeling of being at the top of the world. But as I grew older, mountains became a favorite retreat for meditation.

The Call of the Hills

The distant hills are calling soft;
I crave quiet space with God.
The crowded streets are all too loud;
I need to shed this load.

O how I miss those serene heights
Where winds are calm and still,
Where eagles spread their wings and perch
On rocks high on the hill.

I miss the peace and solitude,
Quiet moments by the stream
Where I first heard the still, small voice
Whispering as in a dream.

I need secluded time to dream;
The hills keep drawing me.
My heart is yearning for the heights—
Up on the hills I'm free.

I will lift up my eyes to the hills—from whence comes my help? My help comes from the Lord, Who made heaven and earth.
—Psalm 121:1, 2

The Peace of the Mountain

I stand high on the mountain
That overlooks the seas.
Something about its stillness
Sets my tense heart at ease.

I love these stately boulders,
Reposed, come rain or wind.
Often when courage fails me,
They flash back on my mind.

O how I love these summits,
The carefree atmosphere.
I feel so close to heaven
Each hour I linger here.

I thank God for this mountain;
Now I descend to rest,
But I've absorbed its stillness;
Its peace reigns in my breast.

You will keep him in perfect peace, whose mind is stayed on You, because he trusts in You.
–Isaiah 26:3

Hills to Climb

So long as day unfolds new dreams,
So long as I have life and breath,
There'll be steep mountains I must climb,
Some peaks to scale to prove my worth.

How could I reach those lofty heights
If I just seek the gentle plain?
I need the path that climbs uphill
To give the soul a prize to gain.

So long as time endures on earth,
A winding path will rise ahead:
I'll never lack a hill to climb—
Each summit reached, my fears are shed.

After climbing a great hill, one only finds that there are many more hills to climb.
—Nelson Mandela

Interlude: On the Shores of Galilee

The sea is calm this morning. A solemn stillness pervades the atmosphere. I feel a deep peace as I walk along the shores of Galilee.

What a privilege to walk where Jesus walked! Just visiting Capernaum and seeing ruins of the ancient synagogue where Jesus preached leave me convinced that Christ is real. He isn't just a myth.

Jesus performed some of His greatest miracles right here. Great multitudes came from Judea, Jerusalem, and other cities seeking healing: "And the whole multitude sought to touch Him, for power went out from Him and healed them all" (Luke 6:19). No invalid went back still groaning after meeting Jesus. How I wish I had been here between 27 and 31 AD! I imagine myself as part of the crowd, eager to meet Jesus face to face. What would I have discussed with Him?

> I imagine myself as part of the crowd, eager to meet Jesus face to face.

I think I'd have been a little timid to approach Him at first. Being in the presence of One who knows my vilest thoughts and actions would have unsettled me. But hearing Him saying to some notorious sinner in the crowd, "Son, be of good cheer. Your sins are forgiven," would have emboldened me. I'd have pressed my way through the crowd to embrace Him. *Will He push me back?* I'd wonder. But deep down I'd know He wouldn't. Unlike some in the crowd, I wouldn't use this great opportunity to ask for bread or riches. My deepest hunger isn't for physical but spiritual blessings.

I long for a deeper relationship with God. I long for the peace that comes from knowing that all is well between me and the Savior. I would have begged for a very private moment with Him, like Nicodemus did. There are matters of salvation I'd have wanted settled. He wouldn't deny me the privilege.

But now Christ is not physically here in Capernaum anymore. He has ascended into heaven. Even so, He invites me to "come boldly to the throne of grace, that we may obtain mercy and find grace to help in time of need" (Heb. 4:16). So I still have access to Christ. I've better access to Him today than I'd have had if I'd lived in Capernaum two thousand years ago.

No need to make wearisome pilgrimages to find Jesus. No need to press through a hostile crowd that might not have been welcoming to me. Now, I can reach Jesus anytime I need Him. Today He invites me to cast all my cares upon Him. That's why I have this deep peace.

A Dream

One night I wandered in my dream
Through ancient Galilee.
I mingled with the sick, who cried,
"Have mercy, Lord, on me."

I saw the Healer drawing near,
Moved by their deep despair.
He touched the leper's festering sores,
Cured him with tender care.

He heard the blind man's plaintive plea
And touched his darkened eyes.
I saw wild rapture in the crowd,
Their sudden, glad surprise.

I too had yearned for healing grace
To cure the rot within.
I cried, "Have mercy on me, Lord.
Wash me from guilt and sin."

He smiled and whispered, "Son, cheer up.
I've washed the sin away."
I walked from ancient Galilee,
Humming "O Happy Day."

Then behold, they brought to Him a paralytic lying on a bed. When Jesus saw their faith, He said to the paralytic, "Son, be of good cheer; your sins are forgiven you."
–Matthew 9:2

Emotional Healing

As I launch out this morning,
Racing against the clock,
I plead the Spirit's presence
To guide and guard my walk:

Tame all my wild emotions,
As restless as the sea.
Restrain mood swings and tempers;
From impulse set me free.

God, heal the nervous system,
Restore calm in my world,
Erase the scars of trauma;
Your healing touch afford.

Increase my share of patience,
My stock of self-control.
O Grace, restore Christ's image,
Diminished by the fall.

Guard me from harming others
By unkind looks or lies.
Let me not sow division
Or cause a tear to rise.

If friend or foe should hurt me
And daggers stab my soul,
Remind me of dark Calvary;
Sweet Spirit, keep control.

He heals the brokenhearted and binds up their wounds.
–Psalm 147:3

Raining

When it is raining in my world
And thunder fills my mind,
When fields are swamped and plains are drenched,
And peace I cannot find,

I look to You who calmed the storm
That night on Galilee:
When all seemed lost, You raised Your hand
And stilled the raging sea.

I call to You, for there's no name
As powerful as Yours.
It's such a comfort, Lord, to know
Your love forever endures.

This very storm that threatens me—
So wild and out of hand—
Will hush up like a gentle breeze,
Obeying Your command.

*The name of the Lord is a strong tower;
the righteous run to it and are safe.*
–Proverbs 18:10

Interlude: Walter's Miracle Kidney

Narrated by the author. A note to the reader: Walter and I have been very close throughout his trying times.

My world plunged into darkness when my kidneys began to fail. Dialysis became my new routine: three days a week, five hours each session, stretching into the early morning hours. I often returned home at 2:00 a.m., drained of energy and filled with dread. Every minute I felt severe agony. My weight plummeted from 172 pounds to 110, leaving my 5' 11" tall body unrecognizable.

Clearly, I was running out of time. My doctor said my only hope was a kidney transplant. The gravity of my situation hit me hard. Where would I find a donor? In Zimbabwe, organ donation is uncommon.

The future looked terrifying, yet I put my will in place. Every day my family and I pleaded with God for healing. My church gathered around me too, praying for a miracle. Meanwhile, I celebrated the dawn of each new day that God allowed me to live.

My sister, Kudzi, bravely offered to donate. It was the first glimmer of hope after many months of groping in despair. Three lab tests were needed to determine whether her kidney matched. The first two lab tests were done in Zimbabwe and suggested that her kidney might match. But these were only preliminary results. The third, most critical test had to be done in Cape Town, South Africa, at Chris Bernard Memorial Hospital. This test would be more conclusive. I booked my appointment at the renal unit in Cape Town, but just before we left, I got an urgent call from my doctor.

"I'm sitting with a gentleman named Farai in my clinic," he said. "He just walked in and asked me if I knew anyone in need of a kidney. He is offering to donate."

I suspected this "gentleman" was a conman. "How did he know I am looking for a donor?" I asked.

"He didn't know," My doctor explained. "He says he read about organ donation in a magazine and he just wants to save a life."

> I suspected this "gentleman" was a conman. "How did he know I am looking for a donor?"

The coincidence puzzled me. How could I explain the perfect timing? *Is there a divine hand in this?* I wondered.

I still had a sneaking suspicion that Farai would make heavy financial demands in exchange for his kidney, but when I met him, he seemed very pleased that he had found someone in dire need. "This is a *free* donation," Farai confirmed.

My doctor took his blood samples to the lab. Preliminary results showed that his kidneys might match. My doctor then advised me to take both Farai and Kudzi to Cape Town. There, I decided to get Kudzi tested first. The results that came back were devastating: her kidneys were not a match.

I felt I had reached the end of the road. If my sibling's kidney didn't match, how could Farai's? Yet when Farai's results came, his kidneys were a perfect match. Against all odds, God had provided. What an incredible answer to prayer!

More than ten years later, I'm still living a normal life, healthy and strong. I'm now in a support group for kidney patients, sharing my story as a witness to God's miracles.

When I think of Farai, I remember that our faith often fails even when God is clearly demonstrating His guidance, and sometimes answers to prayer come from the most unexpected places. God is still at work even when our faith falters.

The Storm Won't Touch My Heart

Outside a storm is raging—
There's fury in the wind—
Yet here within my parlor,
The storm can't vex my mind.

I see through rattling windows
Trees bending in the blast;
The mighty oak is bending
Beneath each savage gust.

But in my cozy chamber,
A settled peace I find
Where floods that wreak destruction
Won't stress my quiet mind.

I've prayed and sensed God's presence;
Though rocks may rend apart,
I'm cradled in His safety—
The storm won't touch my heart.

---

*He shall cover you with His feathers,
and under His wings you shall take refuge ….*
–Psalm 91:4

In the Morning

Lord, in the morning when I wake,
My thoughts first turn to You;
I seek Your presence through this day
In all I aim to do.

I know not what the rising sun
Has stored up for today,
But so long as You guide my walk,
I'm safe all through the way.

Lord, Your eyes see the furthest end;
My view is clouded here,
So help me trust Your point of view
And walk with greater cheer.

*My voice You shall hear in the morning, O Lord;
in the morning I will direct it to You, and I will look up.*
–Psalm 5:3

Living Waters

God, come into my dehydrated soul
Like gentle summer rain.
My heart is yearning for Your soothing grace—
Come ease this weary pain.

Why should I drink from shallow, stinking wells
When I can draw from You?
God, lead me closer to the living stream,
To fountains that are pure.

Why must I suffer through this long dry patch
While oceans run so deep?
Come, Spirit, quench the dryness in my soul—
In You my trust I'll keep.

> *The Lord will guide you continually, and satisfy your soul in drought, and strengthen your bones; you shall be like a watered garden, and like a spring of water, whose waters do not fail.*
> –Isaiah 58:11

Nature's Healing

My heart felt heavy in my chest
And lifeless as a stone.
Some thoughtless words tossed in my ear
Left me distressed and worn.

"How could a friend betray my trust?"
I cried in deep despair.
All day I harbored vengeful schemes,
All day I whined with care.

But when I climbed the lofty hill
To catch a gentle breeze,
The cooing dove sang to my ear
A message of sweet peace.

I found sweet healing on the hill
Among the humming bees,
Beside the stream that gently flowed
Between the rocks and trees;

And as I mounted down the hill
Glad music filled the air—
I lost the burden that I bore,
The weariness and care.

In the country the sick find many things to call their attention away from themselves and their sufferings. Everywhere they can look upon and enjoy the beautiful things of nature—the flowers, the fields, the fruit trees laden with their rich treasures, the forest trees casting their grateful shade, and the hills and valleys with their varied verdure and many forms of life.
–Ellen White

It Doesn't Pay

I lived my life apart from God;
Vain dreams lured me astray.
But after years of fruitless toil,
I know it doesn't pay.

The call of fame and instant wealth
Enticed my soul away.
A sad harvest of thorns I reaped;
It really didn't pay.

Now, with a sense of deep remorse,
I've come back home to stay.
I've turned my back on foolish pride;
It really didn't pay.

For what will it profit a man if he gains the whole world, and loses his own soul?
–Mark 8:36

Conversion

I'm making changes in my life;
I'll be a brand-new man inside.
I've broken free from carnal chains—
   In faith and trust I now abide.

I've yielded stubborn will to God
   To let His wisdom take control;
My shipwrecked life needs His command—
   O God, be Captain of my soul.

I need far-reaching changes made—
Too long I dwelt in sin's embrace—
O Grace, anoint my heart and mind,
Or else no lasting change takes place.

The Way I Feel

It's not the calm or strife outside
That shapes the way I feel,
For thoughts have power to sway the mood,
To poison or to heal.

A little trust when times are sad
Lights up my gloomy day,
But doubt and fear deep in the mind
Can color all things gray.

I'll dwell on faith and hope today;
I'll cast sad doubts aside.
I'll count the blessings in my store
And not what is denied.

---

*We are not victims of the world we see;
we are victims of the way we see the world.*
–Shirley MacLaine

It's Morning on the Other Side

It is the twilight hour,
The day is passing on;
But not all earth is wrapped in night—
This dusk is somewhere else a dawn.

Beyond horizons deep
The seagulls glide and soar;
They dive and swim beneath the waves
Because it's morning on their shore.

It is the sunset hour,
The clock says eventide;
But ever since this night began
It's daybreak on the other side.

Provision

I've treasured in my memory's bank
Some tidbits from God's Holy Word
In case the way grows long and steep
And I get famished on the road.

I shall draw strength from the rich Book
To take me over barren hills;
I shall find confidence and strength
To mitigate against all ills.

I've stored deep in my soul today
A vast reserve of fortitude;
The storeroom of my mind shall keep
A psalm to cheer in solitude.

And should temptations press me hard,
I shall not yield like other days.
I've stored the sacred Word within
And tuned my heart to sing God's praise.

*Your word I have hidden in my heart,
that I might not sin against you.*
–Psalm 119:11

Be Still

Be still and know that I am God;
Let all your fears release.
Though fortunes fade and turn to dust,
Find solace, rest in peace.

Be still and place your hand in Mine;
Find restful, healing sleep.
Lay down your burdens at My feet;
Trust Me though ways grow deep.

Be still and fear no rising waves;
Rough winds obey My will.
I'm with you till the very end—
Be very calm and still.

Interlude: Where Is Thy Victory?

King Herod arrested Peter, intending to execute him after Passover. The Jewish leaders who had crucified Jesus were baying for Peter's blood, also. On the last night before the planned execution, Peter lay bound in chains between two armed soldiers while "constant prayer was offered to God for him by the church" (Acts 12:5).

What was passing through his mind as he awaited execution? Did he perhaps entertain hope that God would miraculously prevent his death? Very unlikely. Peter still remembered the bloody execution of John the Baptist. Christ could have rescued *him*, but He didn't. Peter also recalled how Christ Himself drained the bitter cup and endured the cross and its agonies. God didn't come to *His* rescue, either. Stephen was brutally stoned to death, and Apostle James beheaded.

In fact, on what should have been a night of terror, Peter fell sound asleep. "Why should I be the exception?" he must have reasoned. In his mind, Peter must have seen his own head decapitated with the sword, but he seemed unperturbed. Why?

After witnessing the resurrection of Jesus, death must have seemed totally robbed of its terror for Peter. I imagine he was in deep thought that night, anticipating his own resurrection. That is why, face to face with his own death, he could sleep in perfect peace.

Facing the Night

The sun is setting in the west,
The woods grow hush and chill.
In just a moment, day will pass
Beyond the clouded hill.

I am not afraid to face the dark;
Let twilight shadows creep.
I know it's time to say goodnight
And close my eyes in sleep.

This sun that's setting in the west
Will rise with morning light.
This thought brings peace as I descend
Into the quiet night.

Do not marvel at this; for the hour is coming in which all who are in the graves will hear His voice and come forth ....
–John 5:28, 29

Interlude: Shall We Live Again?

When the Greek philosopher, Socrates, was awaiting execution, his friends asked him one last question: "Shall we live again?" Socrates responded, "I hope so, but no man can know."

I thank Christ that we can now give a confident "yes" to that question. The great promise of the resurrection has cheered millions on their deathbed. John Donne expressed this hope succinctly when he said, "One short sleep past, we wake eternally / and death shall be no more" ("Death, Be Not Proud").

Beyond the Setting Sun

What lies beyond the setting sun,
Beyond horizons deep?
The dawning of a brand-new day
When nature wakes from sleep.

What lies beyond the dismal gloom
When eyelids close in death?
The resurrection morning bright,
When Christ returns to earth.

No Winter's Chilling Breeze

No winter's chilling breeze will blow
In God's eternal home.
No leaf will wither on its twig
In the sweet age to come.

No broken heart will need repair,
No scar or bleeding sore,
No tears will gather in our eyes—
These clouds shall be no more.

No parting words or farewell songs
With friends we've loved and known.
Eternal spring awaits us there—
This chill will all be gone.

For the Lord Himself will descend from heaven with a shout, with the voice of an archangel, and with the trumpet of God, and the dead in Christ will rise first.
–1 Thessalonians 4:16

Christ Within

When Christ dawns in my heart,
I'm like a little child:
My callous thoughts dissolve and die,
The mood is sweet and mild.

When He is Lord and King,
My whole world is at peace.
He comes with such rich grace and power
All carnal cravings cease.

When Christ reigns in my life,
Discord and woe subside.
He whispers "Peace—be still" to me
When He comes to reside.

Peace I leave with you. My peace I give to you; not as the world gives do I give to you. Let not your heart be troubled, neither let it be afraid.
–John 14:27

The Exit Door

My journey here will soon come to a close;
The music of the world will cease.
All that will matter when life ebbs away
Is quiet conscience that's at peace.

I shall not boast of mansions I have built;
I take no wealth into the grave.
When night comes on, I need peace with my Lord,
For He alone holds power to save.

I want my old accounts paid up in full
When I stand at the exit door.
It shall cheer me to find my record clean—
I shall not be afraid to go.

Climb Your Mountain

Take time to climb your mountain;
The dreamers do and dare.
Set your eyes on the summits—
It's crowded less up there.

The mountain strains your muscles
And makes them tough and strong.
Don't dwell long in the valley
Where all lame ducks belong.

Life is just like a mountain
We all must brave to climb.
From childhood till adulthood,
It's uphill all the time.

My Little Cares

I shall cast at the feet of Jesus
The little cares that weigh me down.
Each anxious thought and pressing worry,
I'll let Him bear them as His own.

I shall kneel at the cross of Calvary
And feel its shadow touch my soul.
Though now I ache with weary burdens,
I shall rise free, restored, and whole.

I'll sit still at the feet of Jesus
And let His peace flow through my veins.
Though undeserving of His favor,
His grace will soothe my deepest pains.

After the Storm

I thank you God that I can smile again
After the wind and rain.
Just yesterday I pleaded for a break,
But torrents lashed the plain.

I thank You for this rainbow in the sky—
This interlude of peace.
The turtledove sings in my ear again,
Setting my soul at ease.

My Heart's Temple

God, cleanse the temple of my heart
As Christ did with the ancient one.
I sense a wicked atmosphere
As Satan seeks to claim Your throne.

My heart is Your great temple, God—
Dethrone demons and seize control.
Let them, like Dagon, fall and break;
Command them all to leave my soul.

Return to Your great temple, God;
You've been absent for far too long.
Sit as Refiner, cleanse my heart,
Restore my faith, and make me strong.

Do you not know that you are the temple of God and that the Spirit of God dwells in you?
–1 Corinthians 3:16

Letting Go

I'm letting go my worrying habit
Just like a bug sheds its old skin.
I'm learning now to trust in Jesus
And free my heart from all my sin.

I'm thrusting all my cares behind me;
Old doubts and fears haunt me no more.
I'm trusting Him who steers the planets
To guide me through the open door.

I'm turning in a new direction,
I need a clearer point of view.
For long I've missed the joy of living—
Today I place my trust in You.

I Will Be There

I will be there when you need me,
And I can lend my hand.
When all your dreams have turned to dust,
Just count on me as a friend.

I will be there when skies grow dark,
And all hope fades away.
You can lean on my shoulder, friend,
When life seems dark and grey.

I've known despair and heartache too,
And I can understand.
I will be there to breathe a prayer
And just walk hand in hand.

Fill My Emptiness

Fill all the vacant spaces in my heart
With Your rich presence, Lord.
Replace the craving for material things,
The things I seek to hoard.

Come quench the hungers I have felt for long—
A famine grips my soul—
Come like the rain on parched and barren fields,
Refresh and make me whole.

You promised those who drink from Your deep well
Will never crave again.
This emptiness consumes my inner strength—
Come now, or life feels vain.

My Heart Is Like a Fortress

My heart is like a fortress
Where earth's fierce conflicts cease.
The Prince of Peace resides there;
He sets my soul at ease.

My heart is like a harbor,
The place of safe retreat.
The Master calms anxiety;
I'm safe though strong tides beat.

My heart is like a tower,
Serene while billows roll.
Each time I feel His presence,
It's calm deep in my soul.

The Windows of Your Heart

Open the windows of your heart
And let the fresh air drift.
You've shut them tight; now welcome in
A breeze that will uplift.

Sweep out cold prejudice and hate.
Why linger long in gloom?
Let bright rays from the Son break through
And light the darkened room.

Open the windows wide to grace,
Let love's sweet spirit flow;
Draw back the curtain of your soul
And let broad daylight show.

No soul thrives in a shadowed space;
Embrace the sunny view.
Open your heart to warmth and light
And find renewal true.

Like the Rose

Love, like the rose, blooms in the sun—
The sunshine of your smile—
But petals wither fast and die
When words turn harsh and vile.

Love cannot thrive in hostile climes
Amid relentless blame.
Only thorns grow on rocky ground;
No rose can bloom the same.

Love shrivels in cold, selfish hands
That take but never give,
So make your heart a garden fair;
Love needs light to survive.

New Beginning

Begin this day by turning to the Lord
As sunflowers seek the morning sun.
Let not the memories of old sins haunt you—
God laid them all upon His Son.

Did you defame your name with sinful deeds?
Plead for His mercy and forget.
Did you stumble and crash the dream you held?
This day holds splendid visions yet.

God grants a new beginning to the world
With every rising of the sun.
Lift up your eyes and seek renewing grace—
The Lord will not begrudge His own.

Confidence

I'll greet the dawn with songs of cheer
And trust the sun will shine.
With steadfast heart and lifted head,
I claim this day as mine.

My mind shapes how my world unfolds,
And life grants what I ask.
Though clouds may form and storms may rise,
I'll focus on my task.

I trust in One who stretched the skies
And placed the stars in space.
In God's vast space, no chaos reigns;
His presence fills each place.

Though waves may rise and wind may roar,
I stand within His grace.
Beneath His watch no harm can come;
I rest in His embrace.

Let Me Live Beautifully

Let me live beautifully for one brief hour,
   Just like the rainbow in the sky.
In this swift moment, let me touch one heart
   And dry tears from a weeping eye.

Let me live bountifully in my little space—
   The world is weary from despair—
I can give hope by holding feeble hands;
   A warm embrace can show I care.

O God, connect me with the hungry poor;
   How dare I turn and look away?
It takes so little to relieve their pain;
   Let me reach out without delay.

Let me be pleasant like the roadside flower,
   Ready to cheer a gloomy face.
Tonight let me look back and humbly say
   I made my world a better place.

Building Bridges

I dream of building a long bridge
To span the chasm wide;
The chasm which we caused to be
Through vanity and pride.

The gulf between the races yawns
So wide, so vast, so deep.
A bridge could heal this widening breach;
O how our God must weep.

The gap between the classes looms;
The wealthy scorn the poor.
A bridge must mend this gaping wound,
uniting friend and foe.

O God, make us bridge builders now
To cross this great divide;
Unite us as one family
Together at Your side.

Building Again

The little plan I drew up
And held close to my heart,
The little dream I clung to
Crashed down and blew apart.

The years of precious labor
Were wasted in a day
When castles I constructed
All crumbled into clay.

But I'm not ruined and hopeless;
I've learned from past mistakes.
I'll rise up from the ashes,
No matter what it takes.

God who inspired my vision
Will guide me through the pain,
So I'll launch out with courage—
I trust Him not in vain.

The Light of Yesterday

When I am in distress of mind
And groping in the night,
I look back to the shining spot
Where I last saw the light.

And as I dwell on happy times,
The light of yesterday
Dispels the darkness from my world,
And I can find my way.

When I Get Home at Eventide

When I get home at eventide,
I fling all cares behind.
It's time to join with family
And just unpack the mind.

Home is the place where love begins;
I find acceptance here.
Away from harsh and hostile streets,
I'm free from every fear.

Home is the place where hopes and dreams
Are born and nurtured well;
A little paradise on earth
Where children can excel.

I love the little cozy place
That I can call my own.
When I roam far from home I miss
These pleasures I have known.

When I get home at close of day,
I feel such sweet welcome.
I hold the treasures of the heart,
For there's no place like home.

The World Needs You

Though crowded earth may sometimes seem,
Your role is needed still.
God planned your birth before the sun
To fit His perfect will.

You're not a random stroke of fate—
Stand tall and do not fear.
Before the dawn of time, God set
Your purpose to be clear.

If you would rise and boldly say,
"God needs me on this earth,"
We'd make this world a better place
Where all could find their worth.

I sense within my very soul
God called me to this time.
My role seems small, yet vast it is
In His grand paradigm.

X-Ray Eyes

I often long for X-ray eyes
To see the heart's deep pain.
I only see tears in the eyes
And wonder what they mean.

God, help me view the fragile heart
Where tears are rising from.
Unveil the fractures deep inside;
Make me a healing balm.

God, let me touch one ailing soul
And brighten drooping eyes.
Perhaps a kind word may provide
More than what money buys.

How dare I pass with unseeing eyes
The pain no smiles can hide?
O touch my heart with grace divine
And rid me of cold pride.

Bear one another's burdens, and so fulfill the law of Christ.
–Galatians 6:2

I Stand So Tall

I stand so tall upon my knees
When seeking God's forgiving grace.
I fall down weak but rise up strong;
In His embrace I find my place.

The prince of darkness feels the threat
When trembling on my knees I plead.
I'm like a giant, invincible;
God frees my soul in time of need.

I fall down helpless at His feet
When all around seems dark and wrong.
God lifts me high above the fray—
When I am weak, then I am strong.

> … My grace is sufficient for you, for
> my strength is made perfect in weakness.
> –2 Corinthians 12:9

The Setting Sun

The sun descends into a golden sky
And evening shadows softly start to fall.
Its parting rays burst through the broken clouds,
Painting a golden dusk to grace us all.

I pause a while to watch the twilight glow;
God's master touch to gracefully end the day.
My thoughts turn inward as the sun goes down:
Will my last moments shine with such display?

This golden scene is etched upon my mind.
O God, at twilight of my life draw near.
Send gentle clouds to showcase grace to all,
But guide me through my sunset free from fear.

*So teach us to number our days, that we
may gain a heart of wisdom.
—Psalm 90:12*

It Takes So Little

It takes so little effort
To mend a broken heart;
You need no thread or needle
To fix the ruptured part.

A gentle touch of kindness,
A soft and tender gaze
Can soothe the keenest aching
And brighten clouded days.

A whispered word of solace
Dropped softly in the ear
Can calm dark fears within me
And wipe away a tear.

It takes so little effort
To calm a weeping child,
Or free a caged-up songbird
And set it to the wild.

> *The Lord God has given Me the tongue of the learned, that I should know how to speak a word in season to him who is weary ….*
> *–Isaiah 50:4*

Healing Light

The sun bestows its healing light
And purges viruses.
They can't survive the sun's full glare
To cause harm and disease.

But greater still, the Son's pure light
Exposes hidden sin.
He penetrates our darkest thoughts
And cures the lust within.

O Light Divine, shine in my heart;
Illuminate my soul.
My heart of darkness craves Your light—
Touch me and make me whole.

God, in the chamber of my heart
Where evil still holds sway,
Shine Your light there eternally
And banish night away.

But to you who fear My name The Sun of Righteousness shall arise with healing in His wings ….
–Malachi 4:2

Interlude: East from West

Tendai opened my office door without knocking. Before saying a word, he collapsed onto the floor and burst into tears. Tendai was a senior student at the university where I served as pastor. I thought he had received news from home that a parent or a sibling had died. When he regained his composure, I inquired gently what had happened.

"Yesterday I sneaked out of my room and went to the city to commit suicide. But just before I jumped in front of a fast moving car, a voice commanded me, "Stop! Go and speak to your pastor."

"Why did you want to commit suicide?" I asked softly.

After a long pause, he explained the circumstances. "I did some terrible things in life. I joined a Satanist cult. When I gave it up, I fasted and prayed for forgiveness. For a whole month I fasted. But I did not receive forgiveness."

I drew closer to him and asked. "Who told you that you were not forgiven?"

He paused and then responded, "I did not *feel* forgiven."

"Oh, I see." I responded. "Can you explain to me how forgiveness is felt? I have never felt it either."

Tendai couldn't explain. I had asked him this precisely so that he could understand the futility of basing his Christian experience on feelings.

I looked him straight in the eye. "Have you read God's promises of forgiveness?"

"No, I haven't," he said.

I gave him a pen and a clean sheet of paper. "I am going to read God's promises to you. Write them down."

I started with my favorite, 1 John 1:9: "If we confess our sins, He is faithful and just to forgive our sins and to cleanse us from all unrighteousness." Then I shared Psalm 103:12: "As far as the east is from the west, so far has He removed our transgressions from us."

After I read this Psalm to him, Tendai burst into tears again. But this time, they were tears of relief.

The next day Tendai came back with an exciting testimony. "Yesterday, when I walked into the dormitory after our prayer, my friends said they noticed peace and joy in my countenance. They were all asking me, 'Tendai, what happened to you today?'" A change had come over him. Instead of checking with his feeling to confirm his relationship with God, he had learned to depend on God's promises for his life.

Friend of Sinners

Dear Jesus, friend of sinners,
I come just as I am:
Dehumanized and broken—
Yet You love me the same.

Your grace is more abundant
Than waters of the sea,
And it is just as constant
As air surrounding me.

Then why should I feel hopeless,
A chained and helpless slave,
When grace can break my fetters;
The wretched You can save?

Submerge me in Your mercy
And wash away my shame;
Restore me to Your favor
And rid my soul of blame.

*For by grace you have been saved through faith,
and that not of yourselves; it is the gift of God.
–Ephesians 2:8*

Turning to the Light

As lilies turn to light each day,
So, Lord, I turn to You—
Refresh my spirit, cleanse my heart
Like drops of morning dew.

Instill in me such gentleness
That all I meet may see
Your matchless grace and comeliness,
Reflected clear in me.

Let me this morning spread Your light
To brighten far and near,
That those who journey near my path
May go with greater cheer.

> But we all, with unveiled face, beholding as in a mirror the glory of the Lord, are being transformed into the same image from glory to glory, just as by the Spirit of the Lord.
> –2 Corinthians 3:18

If Jesus Came to Visit

If Jesus came to visit me,
One full day as my guest,
What joy to welcome Him within:
The answer to my quest.

How would I act throughout that day
With Christ here in my home?
With open arms I'd welcome Him,
As well as those who roam.

I would not waste a single hour
Just lost in idle thought,
But seek out those in deep distress
And serve them as I ought.

I'd share warm bread with needy ones,
Their hungry souls to fill,
And weary hearts so worn with care
Could find sweet comfort still.

I'd tell my friends how much He cares,
How freely He forgives.
His love would heal their brokenness;
They'd know my Savior lives.

But Christ, You're present here right now,
You're always by my side.
Help me reflect Your boundless grace
And in Your love abide.

Stay Close to Me

Stay close to me—the way grows steep—
Just like my shadow, linger near;
And when I wander from Your path,
Pursue me still, and draw me near.

Draw close, O God, my heart is weak—
I drift like leaves in autumn wind—
Let me sense You at every turn;
Put guardrails on my wandering mind.

Stay close when pride says I'm secure,
When I feel I don't need you here.
Reveal Yourself, like Jacob saw
That night alone in deep despair.

Draw even closer when I fall—
Without Your help, how can I rise?—
The archfoe waits to steal my soul,
But save me when the tempter tries.

I Need You

I need you in the morning
When day is at its start.
My world is robbed of sunshine
Without you in my heart.

Abide with me at noontide
When burdens weigh me low.
Your presence makes my journey
A lighter path to go.

Draw closer at the twilight
When evening firelight gleams;
And when I rest in slumber,
Visit me in my dreams.

Words You Speak

You never know when you spread tales
How far the whispers go,
For gossip finds swift wings to fly
To places you won't know.

Like arrows shot, your thoughtless tale
May pierce a trusting friend
Or strike the heart, inflicting wounds
That fester, slow to mend.

But kindly words dropped from your tongue,
Coated with healing balm—
How sweet they linger in the heart
And bring both peace and calm.

A Letter to My Unborn Child

I'm writing this while you're as yet unborn,
Still cradled in the womb's embrace.
We're yet to meet, but know that you belong;
A precious gift of loving grace.

You'll make your loud entrance into our world,
Unsure of what the years may hold,
But God who formed you holds the master key
To riches pure and joys untold.

Our world is harsher than the womb's soft touch,
A place of clouded skies and rain,
Yet peace awaits you, child, as you will learn
When God walks with you through the plain.

And so fear not the unknown ways ahead:
You will not walk life's road alone.
God's hand will guide you through life's tangled paths,
And He will not forsake His own.

TEACH Services, Inc.
P U B L I S H I N G

We invite you to view the complete
selection of titles we publish at:
www.TEACHServices.com

We encourage you to write us
with your thoughts about this,
or any other book we publish at:
info@TEACHServices.com

TEACH Services' titles may be purchased in
bulk quantities for educational, fund-raising,
business, or promotional use.
bulksales@TEACHServices.com

Finally, if you are interested in seeing
your own book in print, please contact us at:
publishing@TEACHServices.com
We are happy to review your manuscript at no charge.

www.ingramcontent.com/pod-product-compliance
Lightning Source LLC
Chambersburg PA
CBHW071216160426
43196CB00012B/2325